First published in Great Britain in 1989 by
Belitha Press Limited
31 Newington Green, London N16 9PU

Printed in the UK for Imago Publishing

Bottomley, Jane, *1956-*
Today I am – a cat.
I. Title
823.'914 [J]

ISBN 0-947553-33-9

Today I am . . .

A Cat

by Jane Bottomley

Belitha Press

Good morning Sam.

Today I am . . .

A cat!

How about that?

I will drink my milk from a dish
on the floor,

then I'll wash my chin with a swish
of my paw.

I can chase round the house

and play 'catch' with my mouse . . .

until it won't go any more.

After lunch we go to see Gran.

She's fond of cats,
unlike Aunty Ann.

The thing is, you see,
she is fonder of me . . .

As Gran strokes my fur,
I'll miaow and I'll purr,

or I'll take a short nap
as I curl on her lap.

Then we eat up the cakes
that Gran always bakes,

before saying goodbye,
trying hard not to cry.

It's getting quite dark
going home past the park.

Now the cats on the wall
are beginning to call . . .

And I'm rather glad
that I'm me, after all.